VEGAN MEXICAN COOKBOOK:

Simple Mexican Cookbook For Vegans

By
KATYA JOHANSSON

TABLE OF CONTENTS

INTRODUCTION _____ 5

CHAPTER 1: STARTERS AND SOUPS _____ 7

Black Bean Salsa _____ 7

Pico de Gallo - Authentic Mexican Salsa _____ 8

Fresh and Easy Guacamole Recipe _____ 9

Guacamole with Mayonnaise _____ 10

Taco Salad with Salsa Baked Tofu _____ 11

Taco cheddar _____ 13

Seasoned Roasted-Corn Salad Cups _____ 15

Grilled Veggie Mexican Chopped Salad _____ 17

Mexican Fiesta Pasta Salad _____ 19

Spinach Salad with Salsa Baked Tofu _____ 21

Vegan Taco Salad Recipe _____ 23

Mexican Quinoa Salad _____ 24

Spinach Enchilada Recipe _____ 26

White Beans and Spinach Enchiladas _____ 29

Roasted Corn Quesadillas _____ 32

Black Bean and Salsa Soup _____ 33

Mexican Rice Soup _____ 34

Mexican sweet potato, chili & lime soup _____ 36

Mexican vegetable soup _____ 38

Mexican Minestrone_____ 40

Nacho Soup _____ 41

Sopa-De-Queso _____ 43

Chili Bean Soup _____ 44

Green Pea and Corn Soup _____ 46

CHAPTER 2: MAIN DISHES _____ 47

Red Bean Casserole _____ 47

Red Beans & Rice_____ 48

Mexican Cabbage_____ 50

6-Layer Mexican Pinwheels_____ 52

Vegan Black Bean & Seitan Tamale Pie _____ 54

Vegan Mexican Pizza _____ 56

Mexican Street Corn_____ 58

Mexican Black Bean Stew Recipe with Amaranth Grain _____ 59

Mexican Cauliflower _____ 61

Vegan Mexican Quinoa Bowl _____ 63

Beer Bean-Stuffed Peppers _____ 65

Sweet Potato Burritos _____ 67

CHAPTER 3: DESSERTS _____ 69

Minted Poached Peaches _____ 69

Chocolate-Covered Bananas _____ 71

Vegan Mexican Chocolate Sweet Potato Pudding_____ 72

Mexican Chocolate Cake_____ 74

Mexican Chocolate Cupcakes _____ 76

Mexican Chocolate Lime Pudding Tarts_____ 78

Arroz con Leche {Mexican Rice Pudding} _____ 81

Mexican Chocolate Ice Cream _____ 83

Vegan Empanadas de Calabaza _____ 84

ONE LAST THING... _____ 87

INTRODUCTION

Mexican food history has acquired many cultural influences, improving and reforming the Mexican cuisine with delicious dishes.
That's the reason that Mexican food is so varied, rich and colorful, spicy, and full of flavor..

There are many options for vegetarians in Mexican food like antojitos which are little cravings, quick, inexpensive snacks.

Usually they are livening up with common toppings like a great variety of salsas: chopped onion, cilantro (coriander), lettuce, cabbage, and crema (Mexican sour cream).

The main meal of the day in Mexico is between 2-5pm in the afternoon when restaurants serve "comida corrida" set meals consisting of soup, a main dish, dessert, and agua fresca (water).

Tacos are small soft corn tortillas with any kind of fillings.
Quesadillas are the most common vegetarian option. A quesadilla is a wheat tortilla or a corn tortilla filled with cheese, and/or vegetables, often cooked on a griddle, and then folded in half to form a half-moon shape. In Mexico City they usually deep-fry their quesadillas, making them more like empanadas.

Empanadas are stuffed pastries with fillings such as onion, cheese, spinach, corn, and potato.

Tostadas meaning "toasted".in Spanish. In Mexico some local dishes which are toasted or use a toasted ingredient are called tostadas.

Sopes are small disks of thick fried masa dough with pinched sides to keep the toppings on top like cheese, beans and squash blossom.
Flautas are tortillas filled, rolled and deep-fried. Vegetarian fillings are potato or cheese, and they are usually topped with crema, salsa, lettuce and cheese.

Enchiladas are rolled tortillas, filled with vegetables or panela cheese and covered with salsa.

Mexico is in general a meat focused country like Latin America and vegetarianism isn't mostly appreciated or widespread, but luckily vegetarian ingredients like corn tortillas, beans, cheese, and vegetables feature in many dishes make Mexico a vegan paradise.

CHAPTER 1: STARTERS AND SOUPS

BLACK BEAN SALSA

Ingredients

- About 5 cups cooked black beans, or 3 14-ounce cans black beans, rinsed and drained
- 2 ears of corn, shucked, or 1 can of organic corn, drained
- 6 medium tomatoes, chopped, or about 30 ounces of canned chopped tomatoes, drained
- 2 bunches green onions, chopped
- 2 limes, juiced
- Fresh cilantro, chopped. I love cilantro so I use quite a bit, about half a bunch's worth.
- White wine vinegar, to taste
- Jalapeño (fresh or pickled) and or Fresno peppers

Directions

1. Toss all the ingredients into a big bowl, mix it up and chill for several hours. The longer, the better.

PICO DE GALLO - AUTHENTIC MEXICAN SALSA

Ingredients

- 3 large diced tomatoes
- 1 diced medium sized onion
- 1/4 bunch of cilantro (use more or less depending on your taste)
- juice of half a lemon
- 1/2 tsp. of minced garlic
- 1 tsp of salt
- 2 jalapenos (or more if you prefer it hotter)

Directions

1. Wash tomatoes and cilantro.
2. Dice tomatoes, onions, chop cilantro, jalapenos, and the optional ingredients (avocado, cucumber)
3. Put ingredients in a bowl.
4. Add salt, garlic, the juice of half a lemon. Mix it up and serve.
5. Heat up a frying pan or skillet on medium high heat.
6. Place whole tomatoes in the cookware and toast the outside of it until the skin begins to break and split apart.
7. Remove from heat and continue with step two.

FRESH AND EASY GUACAMOLE RECIPE

Ingredients

- 1 bunch cilantro, leaves only (about 1/2 cup, coarsely chopped)
- 1 jalapeno pepper, minced fine (if you don't like heat, you can either omit this or just use about half of a pepper)
- 2 garlic cloves pressed or minced
- 1/2 cup red onion, diced small
- juice from 1 lime (fresh is best, but you can use about 2 tablespoons bottle lime juice, if needed)
- 4 medium tomatoes, diced
- 4 avocados, diced

Directions

1. In a large bowl, combine the cilantro, jalapeno pepper, garlic, red onion and lime juice.
2. Add chopped tomatoes and mix.
3. Gently fold in the diced avocados.
4. Most guacamole recipes call for smashing the avocado, but if you have beautiful avocados, dice them rather than smashing them.
5. Transfer your prepared guacamole to a serving bowl, if desired, and serve with fresh veggies or tortilla chips.

GUACAMOLE WITH MAYONNAISE

Ingredients

- 2 ripe avocados
- 1 tbsp. lime or lemon juice
- 1/2 tsp. chili powder
- 1 tsp. hot sauce
- 3 tbsps. mayonnaise
- 1 glove garlic, minced
- 1/4 tsp salt
- fresh chopped cilantro (optional)
- 1 tomato, diced small (optional)

Directions

1. Mash together the avocado and lime or lemon juice using a fork until avocado is smooth.
2. Whisk in the other ingredients until smooth, adding fresh cilantro and stirring in the tomatoes last.
3. You could also make this using a food processor.

TACO SALAD WITH SALSA BAKED TOFU

Ingredients

- 2 handfuls of baby spinach, torn if the leaves are large
- 1 medium handful organic tortilla chips, broken into bite-sized pieces (I recommend Que Pasa organic lightly salted tortilla chips)
- 1-2 tbsps. hummus (I use Fontaine Sante roasted garlic flavour)
- 1-2 tbsps. salsa
- approximately 1/4 cup beans (chickpeas or black beans)
- 1/4 avocado, diced
- 1 thick slice of tomato, diced
- 1 thin slice of red onion, cut in half
- 1/4 recipe salsa baked tofu (Short on time? Follow these quick instructions)
- sprinkle of cheddar-style daiya shreds

Directions

1. In a wide bowl or plate, lay down 2 handfuls of spinach.
2. Mix in your broken up tortilla chips into the top layers of the spinach.
3. Layer an even sprinkle of chickpeas, followed by diced tomato, diced avocado, sliced red onion, hot or chilled salsa baked tofu, and a sprinkle of cheddar-style daiya shreds.

4. Serve with a dollop of hummus and salsa on the side.
5. Mix the salsa and hummus into the salad.

TACO CHEDDAR

Ingredients

- 1 tbsp. olive oil
- 1 small onion
- 1 medium red pepper
- 1 tsp. chili powder
- salt
- 1 can black beans or other favorite beans
- 2 plum tomatoes
- ¼ c. fresh cilantro leaves
- 8 flour tortillas
- 3 cups thinly sliced romaine lettuce
- ½ cups shredded Monterey Jack or mild Cheddar cheese

Directions

1. In 12-inch nonstick skillet, heat oil on medium 1 minute.
2. Add onion, pepper, chili powder, and 1/4 teaspoon salt.
3. Cook 10 minutes or until onion and pepper are tender, stirring occasionally.
4. Stir in beans, tomatoes, and cilantro, and cook 3 to 4 minutes to heat through, stirring occasionally.
5. Just before serving tacos, place stack of tortillas between paper towels on microwave-safe plate.
6. Heat in microwave on High 10 to 15 seconds to warm.

7. To serve, divide romaine lettuce and bean mixture among tortillas, top with Monterey Jack cheese, and fold over to eat out of hand.

Seasoned Roasted-Corn Salad Cups

Ingredients

- 3/4 tsp sweet paprika
- 1/2 tsp light-brown sugar
- 3/4 tsp chopped fresh thyme leaves
- Coarse salt
- 6 ears corn, shucked
- 1/2 jicama, peeled and cut into 1/2-inch pieces (2 cups)
- 2 small poblano chilies, seeded, stemmed, and cut into 1/2-inch pieces (1 cup)
- 1/2 cup packed fresh cilantro leaves
- 3 tbsp. extra-virgin olive oil
- 4 1/2 ounces queso fresco, crumbled (1 cup)
- 1 tablespoon fresh lime juice
- 1 cup sour cream

Directions

1. Stir together paprika, sugar, thyme, and 1 1/2 teaspoons salt.
2. Char corn over the flame of a gas stove or in a broiler, turning with tongs, until blackened and blistered, about 3 to 4 minutes each.
3. Let cool, then cut kernels into a large bowl.
4. Toss with jicama, chiles, cilantro, oil, cheese, and lime juice.
5. Season lightly with salt.
6. Place 1 tablespoon sour cream in each of eight 1-cup glasses.

7. Sprinkle each with 1/4 teaspoon paprika mixture.
8. Fill each with 3/4 cup corn salad.
9. Top with remaining sour cream and paprika mixture and serve.

Grilled Veggie Mexican Chopped Salad

Ingredients

- 2-3 heads of romaine washed and chopped
- 1-2 large zucchini grilled and chopped
- 1-2 large summer squash grilled and chopped
- ½-1 red bell pepper grilled and chopped
- ½-1 red onion grilled and chopped
- 1-2 avocado
- ¼ head red cabbage chopped

Ingredients for Grilled Corn Salsa

- 1-2!ears of corn grilled and stripped from the cob
- 2 tbsp. red onion finely chopped
- 1 tomato chopped
- 2-3 tbsp. cilantro chopped
- ¼ tsp red pepper

Ingredients for Seasoned Black Beans

- Black beans 1 can drained
- ¼ cup water
- 1-2 tbsp. red onion, chopped
- ½ tsp season salt
- 1 tsp cumin

Directions for Seasoned black beans

1. In a small saucepan, add the drained rinsed black beans, water, onion, seasoned salt and cumin.
2. Bring to low boil. Cover and reduce heat.
3. Cook 5 minutes.
4. 2.While beans are cooking make the grilled corn salsa:

Directions for Grilled Corn Salsa

1. Using a large sharp knife, remove the corn kernels from the cob. Add them to a bowl.
2. Add chopped red onion, cilantro and tomatoes.
3. Add red pepper to your taste.
4. Using veggies that have already been grilled:
5. Clean and chop the lettuce, add it to a large bowl.
6. Chop the zucchini, squash, bell pepper and onion into bite size pieces and add to the lettuce.
7. Chop the cabbage and slice the avocado. Top lettuce.
8. Add grilled corn salsa and black beans.
9. Use your favorite salsa or chimichurri sauce for dressing!

Mexican Fiesta Pasta Salad

Ingredients

- 1 (16 ounce) package dried rotini pasta
- 1 1/2 cups medium chunky salsa
- 1 cup mayonnaise
- 1/2 cup sour cream
- 1 (16 ounce) can black beans, rinsed and drained
- 1 (11 ounce) can Mexican-style corn with red and green peppers, drained
- 1/2 cup chopped red bell pepper
- 2 green onions, sliced thin
- 1 (4.25 ounce) can sliced black olives, drained
- 1/2 teaspoon garlic powder
- 1/2 teaspoon ground cumin, or to taste
- 1/2 teaspoon dried cilantro, or to taste
- 1 tsp salt
- ground black pepper to taste
- Add all ingredients to list

Directions

1. Bring a large pot of lightly salted water to a rolling boil; cook the rotini in the boiling water until the pasta is cooked through yet firm to the bite, about 8 minutes.
2. Drain.
3. Rinse under cold running water until completely cooled; drain thoroughly.
4. Whisk the salsa, mayonnaise, sour cream, black beans, Mexican-style corn, red bell pepper, green onions, black olives, garlic powder,

cumin, cilantro, salt, and pepper together in a large bowl.

5. Add the cooled pasta and stir to coat evenly.
6. Cover the bowl with plastic wrap and refrigerate 2 hours to overnight before serving.

SPINACH SALAD WITH SALSA BAKED TOFU

Ingredients for Salsa Baked Tofu

- 1 block of extra-firm tofu, cut into small triangles
- 1/3 cup salsa
- 2 tsp. sriracha, or to taste
- 2 tsp. olive oil
- 2 clove garlic, minced or pressed
- pinch of salt
- 1/8 tsp. ground cumin

Ingredients for Salad

- Spinach
- Black beans
- Chopped tomatoes
- Chopped cucumber
- Shredded carrot
- More salsa
- Squeeze of fresh lime juice

Directions

1. Preheat oven to 425F.
2. Combine all the dressing ingredients in a large glass ovenproof pan.
3. Stir to mix well.
4. Add the tofu slices and stir so that they are evenly coated.

5. Allow to marinate for up to 30 minutes, if possible.
6. When ready, bake for 10 minutes, flip and bake 10 minutes more.
7. When ready to make your salad, combine all the salad ingredients and top with the baked tofu.

VEGAN TACO SALAD RECIPE

Ingredients

- 1/3 cup guacamole
- 1/4 cup sour cream
- 2 tablespoons chopped green pepper
- 1 tbsp. chopped green onions
- 1 tbsp. prepared Italian salad dressing
- 1/4 tsp. salt
- 1/4 tsp. chili powder
- 1/4 tsp. pepper
- 3 cups shredded lettuce
- 8 cherry tomatoes, halved
- 1/2 cup canned kidney beans, rinsed and drained
- 1/4 cup sliced ripe olives
- 1/2 cup crushed corn chips
- 1/2 cup shredded cheddar cheese

Directions

1. In a small bowl, combine the first eight ingredients.
2. Set aside.
3. In a large bowl, combine the lettuce, tomatoes, beans and olives.
4. Arrange lettuce mixture on a serving plate.
5. Top with guacamole mixture.
6. Sprinkle with corn chips and cheese.

MEXICAN QUINOA SALAD

Ingredients for salad

- 5-6 cups Mixed Greens
- 1 cup cooked quinoa (red or white)*
- 1/2 cup fresh or canned corn
- 1 cup cooked black beans (seasoned with equal pinches sea salt, cumin, chili + garlic powder)
- 1/4 cup red onion, diced
- 1 orange, segmented
- 1/2 ripe avocado, chopped
- 1/4 cup fresh cilantro, chopped or torn

Ingredients for dressing

- 1/2 ripe avocado
- 1 large lime, juiced (~4 Tbsp)
- 3 Tbsp. orange juice
- 1-2 tsp sweetener of choice (maple syrup, agave, cane sugar, etc.)
- 1-2 tsp. hot sauce
- 1/4 tsp. cumin powder
- 1/8 tsp. chili powder (or sub extra hot sauce or chipotle powder)
- Healthy pinch each sea salt and black pepper
- 1 Tbsp. fresh minced cilantro (optional)
- 3-4 Tbsp. extra virgin olive oil or avocado oil

Directions

1. Begin preparing quinoa first by thoroughly rinsing 1/2 cup quinoa in a fine mesh strainer,

then bringing to a boil with 1 cup water in a small saucepan.

2. Once boiling, reduce heat to simmer, cover and cook on low for 15-20 minutes.
3. Meanwhile, prepare salad ingredients by chopping vegetables, segmenting orange, and warming black beans and seasoning with salt, cumin, chili and garlic powder.
4. Prepare dressing by adding all ingredients to a blender or food processor and blending until creamy and smooth, scraping down sides as needed.
5. Taste and adjust seasonings as needed.
6. Either plate salad and serve with dressing on the side, or toss with dressing before serving.
7. Goes well with salsa, fresh lime juice and tortilla chips.
8. Leftovers keep for up to a few days, though best when fresh.

Spinach Enchilada Recipe

Ingredients

- 3-4 corn or whole wheat tortillas
- 3-4 tbsp. sour cream
- 1/2 cup shredded Mexican/cheddar cheese

Ingredients for the filling

- 1 bunch fresh spinach, cleaned and chopped
- 1 onion, finely chopped
- ½ cup soy granules, soaked in hot water for 10 minutes and drained
- ¼ cup grated paneer
- 1-2 jalapenos, chopped (or to taste)
- 2-3 garlic cloves, finely minced
- 1 tablespoon olive oil
- 2 tsp. cumin seeds
- ½ tsp. black pepper ,freshly cracked
- Salt to taste

Ingredients for the Pico de Gallo (Fresh Tomato Salsa)

- 1 onion, finely chopped
- 1 tomato, finely chopped,
- 1-2 garlic cloves minced
- 1 jalapeno, chopped or use crushed black pepper
- Handful of coriander leaves, chopped
- Juice of 1 large lime
- Salt to taste

Ingredients for the sauce

- 1 heaped tablespoon whole wheat flour
- 2-3 cloves garlic, minced
- 1/2 cup tomato puree
- 2 teaspoon red chili powder
- 2 Chipotle chilies in adobo sauce , finely chopped (optional)
- 1 tbsp. olive oil
- 1 tsp. cumin powder
- ½ tsp. sugar
- About 2 cups vegetable stock
- Salt to taste

Directions for Spinach Enchilada Recipe

1. To begin making the Spinach Enchiladas Recipe, first make the sauce. To do this, blend the Adobo chilies (if desired) with the tomato puree, in a grinder. Set this aside. Place a pan on the heat and warm the oil in it.
2. Sprinkle the flour and sauté until toasty and aromatic. Add the garlic, chili powder, cumin powder and sauté for a 2-3 seconds, before adding the tomato puree, salt, sugar and vegetable stock. Stir together and bring to a boil. Then cook on low heat for 5 minutes.
3. Adjust the consistency of the sauce with stock or water, if required. Then, proceed to make the filling.
4. Place another pan on the heat. Warm some oil and add cumin seeds. Once they sizzle, add the onions, garlic and jalapenos and sauté for 1-2 minutes. Add the spinach and stir. Cook the

spinach until it just wilts. Then, add the soy granules, paneer and season with salt and pepper. Mix well and cook for a minute. Then, take the pan off the heat.

5. The next step is to make the Pico de Gallo. Toss all the ingredients under "For the Pico de Gallo" together in a bowl. To assemble the Enchiladas; grease an 8 inch baking dish. Begin by adding a ladle full of the sauce into the pan and spread it.

6. Warm the Tortillas on a griddle pan or for a minute in the microwave. Then place one tortilla on a flat surface. Spoon in about 2-3 tablespoon of the spinach filling in a line, in the middle of the tortilla. Top it with about a tablespoon Pico de gallo and a table spoon of sour cream. Tightly roll the Tortilla int a tube and place it seam side down in the baking dish.

7. Proceed similarly with all the tortillas, line them up in the baking dish over the layer of the sauce. After all the tortillas are filled and arranged in the baking dish, ladle the sauce on them, till the tortillas are well covered with the sauce. Sprinkle cheese and cover the dish with foil.

8. Bake in a pre-heated oven at 180 degrees C for 30-40 minutes, until the sauce is bubbling. Take it out of the oven and serve hot with Cuban Black Bean Salad

WHITE BEANS AND SPINACH ENCHILADAS

Ingredients for jalapeno sauce

- 3 jalapeno chilies, deseeded and minced
- 1 tbsp. unsalted butter
- 1 tbsp. all-purpose flour
- 3/4 cup vegetable broth
- 1/2 cup sour cream
- 2 garlic cloves, minced
- salt and pepper as needed
- 1/3 cup fresh cilantro, finely chopped

Ingredients for enchiladas

- 2 bunch scallions, chopped greens and white part separated
- 1 small onion, finely chopped
- 2 tbsp. olive oil
- 1 clove garlic, minced
- 3 cups packed spinach, chopped
- 1 tsp. dried oregano
- 1 tsp. lime juice
- 1/4 cup sweet corn
- 1/4 cup white cannelloni beans, drained
- Salt and pepper to taste
- 1/3 cup cilantro, finely chopped
- 5 medium sized flour tortillas
- 1 cup sharp cheddar cheese

Directions

1. To begin making White Beans and Spinach Enchiladas with Spicy Jalapeno Sauce, first preheat oven to 200 degrees C and grease a 9x13 baking tray with some butter or oil or nonstick spray. Place a pan on the heat, with some olive oil and add minced garlic, chopped onion and chopped white portions of scallions to it.
2. Toss it together with some salt and sauté until translucent. Next, add spinach, dried oregano, sweet corn, cannelloni beans and sauté once again. Check for salt and pepper and add as needed. Switch off the heat and add lime juice, cilantro to the spinach mixture. Stir well and keep aside.
3. To prepare the jalapeno sauce, in a sauce pan, melt butter on medium heat, add minced garlic and allow it to sizzle. To this, add flour and cook the butter and flour until slightly brown. Next add vegetable stock little by little, whisking along the way. Pour in the sour cream, add jalapeños and simmer until the sauce thickens into a glossy mix.
4. Season with required salt and pepper.
5. Remove from the heat and add cilantro. The whole process takes about 5 to 6 minutes.
6. To assemble the enchiladas, lay out the tortillas on a flat surface and spoon 1/3 cup beans spinach mixture in the center of each. Sprinkle some cheddar cheese. Roll the tortilla and place seam side down on to the prepared baking dish. Repeat with all remaining tortillas and beans spinach mixture.

7. Pour half of the prepared jalapeño sauce evenly over the top of arranged tortillas. Cover with a foil paper and bake until bubbly. This will take 15 to 20 minutes.
8. Once done pour the remaining jalapeño sauce and sprinkle the scallion greens for garnishing. Serve warm along with some thick cut Potato Wedges, Egg Salad or Spanish Rice

Roasted Corn Quesadillas

Ingredients

- 3 cups Roasted Confetti Corn
- 2 8-oz. balls fresh mozzarella, grated
- 6 8-inch flour tortillas
- 6 Tbs. cilantro leaves, divided, optional
- 1½ cups prepared peach salsa

Directions

1. Combine Roasted Confetti Corn and mozzarella in bowl.
2. Spread heaping 1/2 cup mixture on half of each tortilla, and sprinkle with 1 Tbs. cilantro (optional).
3. Fold tortillas in half over filling.
4. Cook each tortilla in dry skillet over medium heat 2 minutes per side, or until mozzarella has melted and tortillas are crisp and brown.
5. Serve with salsa.

Black Bean and Salsa Soup

- Ingredients

- 2 (15 ounce) cans black beans, drained and rinsed
- 1 1/2 cups vegetable broth
- 1 cup chunky salsa
- 1 tsp. ground cumin
- 4 tbsp. sour cream
- 2 tbsp. thinly sliced green onion
- Add all ingredients to list

Directions

1. In an electric food processor or blender, combine beans, broth, salsa, and cumin.
2. Blend until fairly smooth.
3. Heat the bean mixture in a saucepan over medium heat until thoroughly heated.
4. Ladle soup into 4 individual bowls, and top each bowl with 1 tablespoon of the sour cream and 1/2 tablespoon green onion.

MEXICAN RICE SOUP

Ingredients

- Broth 1 Tbs. olive oil
- 1 small onion, finely chopped (¾ cup)
- 2 cloves garlic, minced (2 tsp.)
- 3 cups low-sodium vegetable broth
- 1 Tbs. grated lime zest
- 1 tsp. dried oregano
- Soup ¼ cup short-grain rice
- 2 small tomatoes, seeded and diced (1 cup)
- ⅓ cup fresh or frozen corn kernels
- 1 8-inch flour tortilla
- 1 avocado, diced (1 cup)
- 2 green onions, thinly sliced (¼ cup)
- ¼ cup chopped cilantro
- 6 lime wedges
- Hot sauce for garnish, optional

Directions to make Broth

1. Heat olive oil in large saucepan over medium heat.
2. Add onion, and sauté 5 to 7 minutes, or until softened. Stir in garlic, and sauté 1 minute more. Add vegetable broth, lime zest, oregano, and 3 cups water.
3. Cover, and reduce heat to medium-low. Simmer 10 minutes. Strain Broth, discard solids, and return to saucepan.

Directions to make Soup

1. Add rice to Broth. Bring to a simmer over medium-low heat, cover, and simmer 15 minutes, or until rice is soft.
2. Stir in tomatoes and corn, and season with salt and pepper. Simmer 10 minutes.
3. Meanwhile, preheat oven to 350°F.
4. Spray flour tortilla with cooking spray, and cut into thin strips. Arrange strips on baking sheet, and bake 5 to 7 minutes, or until tortilla is crisp.
5. Ladle Soup into serving bowls.
6. Garnish with avocado, tortilla strips, green onions, cilantro, lime wedges, and hot sauce, (optional).

MEXICAN SWEET POTATO, CHILI & LIME SOUP

Ingredients:

- 1 X Large Onion, chopped
- 1 tbsp. Oil
- 1 tbsp. Tomato puree
- 1 X Red chili, deseeded and chopped
- 2 Cloves of garlic, crushed
- 1 tsp Ground cumin
- 750g Sweet potato, peeled and cut into even chunks
- 1 Liter Vegetable stock
- Juice of 2 limes
- 4 tbsp. Half-fat crème fraiche
- 4 tbsp. Herb-flavored oil, to serve (optional)

Directions

1. In a large pan heat the onion in the oil, covered but stirring often, until really soft - about 15 minutes.
2. Add the tomato puree for 2 minutes to caramelize, then add the chili, garlic and cumin for 1 minute.
3. Add the sweet potato and stock, bring to a boil, cover and turn down to simmer for 20 minutes, until the potato is tender
4. Allow to cool slightly before whizzing in a food processor (or with a stick blender) until smooth.

5. Add the lime juice, season to taste and warm through.
6. Swirl 1 tbsps. Crème fraiche and herby oil into each bowl of soup then serve.

MEXICAN VEGETABLE SOUP

Ingredients

- 1 tbsp. extra-virgin olive oil
- 1 brown onion, finely chopped
- 2 garlic cloves, crushed
- 2 tsp. dried oregano
- 2 tsp. ground coriander
- 1/4 teaspoon ground chili
- 5 cups chopped vegetables (see note)
- 5 cups vegetable stock
- 400g can diced tomatoes
- 400g can red kidney beans, drained, rinsed
- 125g can corn kernels, drained
- Fresh coriander leaves, to serve
- Lime wedges, to serve
- Grilled flour tortillas, to serve

Directions

1. Heat oil in a large heavy-based saucepan over medium-high heat. Add onion.
2. Cook for 5 minutes or until softened.
3. Add garlic and spices. Cook for 1 minute or until fragrant.
4. Add chopped vegetables. Cook, stirring, for 1 to 2 minutes, to coat.
5. Add stock and tomatoes.
6. Bring to the boil. Reduce heat to medium-low.
7. Simmer, partially covered, for 20 to 25 minutes or until vegetables are tender. Add beans and corn.

8. Cook for a further 5 minutes or until heated through.
9. Season with salt and pepper. Ladle into bowls. Sprinkle with coriander. Serve with lime and tortillas

MEXICAN MINESTRONE

Ingredients

- 1/3 cup cucumber, finely chopped
- 4 1/2 cups Brown Stock
- 3/4 cup boiled sweet corn kernels
- 2 tbsp. sliced mushrooms
- 2 tbsp. chopped onions
- 2 large tomatoes, peeled and chopped
- 1 tbsp. chopped coriander
- 3/4 cup chopped spinach
- 1 tbsp. butter
- salt to taste
- 2 tbsp. grated processed cheese

Directions

1. Put the tomatoes in hot water for 10 minutes. Take out the skin and chop them.
2. Heat the butter and fry the onions for a few seconds.
3. Add the corn, mushrooms and salt and cook for 2 to 3 minutes.
4. Add the tomatoes, spinach, cucumber and brown stock and boil.
5. Serve hot garnished with the coriander and cheese.

NACHO SOUP

Ingredients

- 1/2 cup boiled sweet corn kernels
- 2 cups nachos, refer handy tip
- 5 big sized ripe tomatoes , cut into quarters
- 1/4 cup chopped onions
- 2 tbsp. corn flour
- 1/4 cup grated cottage cheese
- 1/2 vegetarian seasoning cube
- 1/2 tsp sugar
- 2 tbsp. butter
- Salt to taste

Ingredients for the garnish

- 2 tbsp. boiled sweet corn kernels
- 2 tbsp. grated processed cheese

Directions

1. In a pan, add 4 cups of water and tomatoes. Cook till the tomatoes are tender.
2. Blend in a mixer till smooth and pass through a sieve. Keep aside.
3. Heat the butter in a pan, add the onions and sauté till they turn translucent.
4. Mix the corn flour in ½ cup of water.
5. Add the corn flour mixture and tomato purée to the pan and bring to a boil.
6. Add the paneer, corn, seasoning cube, sugar and salt and cook for a few minutes.

7. Just before serving, add the nachos and top with corn and cheese.
8. Serve hot.

SOPA-DE-QUESO

Ingredients

- 1 recipe Basic Brown Stock
- 3 fresh bread slices
- 100 grams grated processed cheese
- salt to taste
- black pepper powder to taste

Directions

1. Put the stock to boil.
2. When it starts boiling, add the bread slices, salt, pepper and three-quarters of the cheese.
3. Boil on a slow flame for 20 minutes.
4. Serve hot, sprinkling the balance cheese.

CHILI BEAN SOUP

Ingredients

- 1 cup canned baked beans
- 6 cups roughly chopped tomatoes
- 1 tbsps. oil
- 1/2 cup finely chopped onions
- 1 cup finely chopped capsicum
- 1/2 cup finely chopped spring onions whites and greens
- 1/2 cup finely chopped tomatoes
- 3 tbsps. white sauce
- 1 tbsps. sugar
- 1 tsp chili sauce
- salt to taste

Ingredients for serving

- grated processed cheese

Directions

1. Combine the tomatoes, 4 cups of water and cook on a medium flame for 8 to 10 minutes.
2. Allow the mixture to cool completely.
3. Blend the mixture in a mixer till smooth and then strain it. Keep aside.
4. Heat the oil in a deep pan; add the onions and sauté on a medium flame for 1 minute.
5. Add the capsicum and spring onion whites and greens and sauté on a medium flame for 1 minute.
6. Add the prepared tomato mixture.

GREEN PEA AND CORN SOUP

Ingredients

- 2 cups fresh green peas
- 1 cup sweet corn 1/2 onion, chopped
- 1 clove garlic crushed
- 1 tsp oil
- salt to taste

Ingredients for serving

- 1/4 cup low fat milk
- 1 tsp. chopped coriander
- 1 tsp. chopped mint leaves

Directions

1. Combine the peas, corn, onion, garlic, salt and 4 cups of water and simmer for 10 minutes or until tender.
2. Cool and blend in a mixer to get a smooth purée.
3. Just before serving, add the milk, coriander, mint and salt and bring to a boil.
4. Serve hot.

CHAPTER 2: MAIN DISHES

RED BEAN CASSEROLE

Ingredients

- 3 Cup (48 tbs.) Cooked long grain brown rice
- 3 Cup (48 tbs.) Cooked red beans
- 1 Cup (16 tbs.), diced Red onion
- 1 Cup (16 tbs.), diced Celery
- 2 tbsp. Fresh parsley
- 3 Large, minced Garlic clove
- Ground pepper To Taste
- 1 Dash Hot sauce
- 1 Dash Mexican seasoning

Directions

1. Preheat the oven to 350 degrees F.
2. Lightly spray a 9 x 13-inch baking dish with vegetable oil.
3. Combine all of the ingredients in a large bowl.
4. Spoon into the prepared casserole dish.
5. Bake uncovered for 20 minutes.
6. Serve hot.

RED BEANS & RICE

Ingredients

- 12 Ounce Red beans, soaked overnight
- 1 Medium Red onion, coarsely chopped
- 16 Ounce Mild salsa
- Cilantro tied to a bouquet
- 1 Large Jalapeno, seeded, cut in half
- 1 Tsp. Ground cumin
- 1 Tsp. Dried oregano
- 1/2 Tsp. Coriander
- 3 Clove (15 gm), Garlic minced
- 1/2 Tsp. Salt
- 1/2 Tsp. Pepper
- 2 Cup (32 tbs) Brown rice
- 4 Cup (64 tbs) Water
- 1 Large Tomato, chopped
- 1 tbsp. Lime juice

Directions

1. In a large pan or crock pot put red beans, onion, salsa, cilantro, jalapeno, cumin, oregano, coriander and garlic.
2. Season with salt & pepper.
3. Bring to a boil, cover and simmer for 5 hours, stirring occasionally.
4. While the beans are cooking, prepare 2 cups of brown rice as per package instructions.
5. When beans are cooked, remove the kitchen twine and the jalapeño pieces.
6. Mix together the beans and rice.

7. Make a salad of chopped tomatoes, chopped cilantro, lime juice and salt.
8. In a serving plate, serve beans and rice topped with tomato salad.

Mexican Cabbage

Ingredients

- ½ whole   cabbage
- 1 whole   sweet onion, diced
- 2 whole   garlic cloves, minced
- 8 ounces   tomato sauce
- 4 ounces   green chills, diced
- 2 tbsp.   tomato paste
- 1 tsp.   cumin
- ½ tsp.   dried oregano
- ¼ tsp.   black pepper
- 1 cup   corn, frozen
- 1 cup   black beans, cooked
- ¼ cup   baked corn chips

Directions

1. Chop cabbage into thin strips, set aside.
2. Line a medium saucepan with water and sauté onions and garlic over high heat until translucent. Add cabbage, tomato sauce, chilies, paste and spices.
3. Reduce heat to medium and cook until cabbage is tender, about 10 minutes.
4. Turn off heat and stir in frozen corn until evenly distributed.
5. Taste, adjusting spices as needed. Salt to taste.
6. Mix in black beans before serving.
7. Break corn tortilla chips into small pieces in your hand and sprinkle over top before serving.

6-LAYER MEXICAN PINWHEELS

Ingredients

- 2 large vegan flour tortillas
- optional: 2/3 cup Spreadable Vegan Mexican Cheese, divided
- 2/3 cup (158 g) vegan refried beans (I love Trader Joe's brand), divided
- 1/2 ripe avocado, finely sliced or diced, divided
- 1/2 cup (80 g) red onion, finely diced, divided
- 1/2 cup (75 g) finely diced tomato or chunky salsa, excess liquid drained, divided
- 1/2 cup (30 g) fresh cilantro, finely chopped, divided

Directions

1. If using the Spreadable Vegan Mexican Cheese, prepare first. Otherwise, move onto the next step.
2. Lay one tortilla flat and spread with a thin layer of spreadable cheese - about 1/3 cup.
3. Next top with ~ 1/3 cup refried beans and spread flat. Continue layering with 1/4 avocado, 1/4 cup onion, 1/4 cup tomato or salsa, and 1/4 cup cilantro.
4. Use your hands to flatten all the ingredients down so it's easier to roll. Then tightly roll from one end to the other and place seam side down on a cutting board. If any ingredients fall out of the tortilla when rolling, it's OK! It's a hefty pinwheel, so just scrape it aside and move along.

5. Starting in the center of the tortilla, use your hands to form and tighten the roll, moving outward toward the edges. This will help the fillings form together and make slicing easier.
6. Use a serrated knife and slice into 1/2-inch slices - about 8-10.
7. Repeat the process with second tortilla and remaining ingredients. You should have ~20 pinwheels.
8. Serve immediately, or cover and refrigerate for up to 2-3 days.

Vegan Black Bean & Seitan Tamale Pie

Ingredients

- 1 T vegetable oil
- 1 yellow onion, diced
- 3 cloves garlic, minced
- 1 jalapeno (seeds and ribs removed, minced)
- 1 T tomato paste
- 2 tsp. chili powder
- 1 tsp. ground cumin
- 1 medium tomato, diced
- 1 green bell pepper, diced
- 1 8 oz. package of seitan, cubed, diced
- ¾ cup cooked black beans
- ½ cup frozen corn kernels
- ½ tsp. salt
- ¼ cup sliced black olives
- ¾ cup shredded non-dairy cheese
- Garnish: plain, nondairy yogurt

Directions

1. Preheat oven to 350 degrees.
2. In a large sauté pan, heat vegetable oil. Add onion, garlic and jalapeno and sauté for about 2 minutes. Stir in tomato paste, chili powder and ground cumin and cook another minute.
3. Stir in tomato and green pepper and cook another 2 minutes. Stir in seitan and black beans and cook another 2 minutes. Stir in corn and salt and cook an additional minute.

4. Remove from heat. Stir in black olives and non-dairy cheese.
5. Prepare half of the vegan cornbread batter recipe (linked above) for the topping. A half recipe covers the dish nicely. Just divide all of the amounts of the ingredients in half and prepare in the same manner to combine the wet and dry ingredients.
6. Set batter aside, and do not bake it according to the cornbread recipe's instructions.
7. Transfer bean mixture into the pie pan. Press mixture down firmly and out to the edges. Pour the cornbread batter evenly over the top of the pie, smoothing out any lumps or bubbles.
8. Bake at 350 degrees about 40 minutes or until the cornbread topping is cooked and a fork test comes out clean.
9. Cut into slices and serve with plain, non-dairy yogurt.

VEGAN MEXICAN PIZZA

Ingredients

- 420g can kidney beans, drained
- 1 tsp. cumin
- 2 garlic cloves
- 2 tsp. smoked paprika
- 1/4 tsp chili powder
- 2 tbsp. lemon juice
- 1 tbsp. olive oil
- Pinch of sea salt
- Pinch of freshly cracked black pepper
- 2 pizza bases
- coriander leaves (to garnish)
- sliced avocado (to garnish)

Ingredients for toppings

- 1/2 red capsicum, thinly sliced
- 2 large tomatoes, thinly sliced
- 15 Kalamata olives, sliced
- 1/2 jalapeno chili, thinly sliced
- 1/2 purple onion, thinly sliced
- 1/2 cup canned corn kernels

Ingredients for Cheesy Sauce

- 1 cup pre-soaked cashews, drained
- 1/4 cup nutritional yeast
- 1 tablespoon lemon juice
- 1 tablespoon olive oil
- Pinch of sea salt
- Pinch of freshly cracked black pepper

- 120ml water

Directions

1. Preheat oven to 200 degrees Celsius and add two pizza bases to pizza trays.
2. In a food processor or blender, add all bean ingredients and process until smooth.
3. Spoon the smooth bean base onto the pizza bases and spread evenly.
4. Top the pizzas bases with the capsicum, tomato, olives, jalapenos, onion and corn.
5. In a food processor or blender, add all "cheesy sauce" ingredients and process until smooth and creamy. Season with more salt and pepper to taste and add more water if you would like a thinner consistency.
6. Drizzle the cheesy sauce on to the pizza bases. Drizzle with a spoon or use a piping bag like I did. Add as much or as little cheesy sauce as desired. Refrigerate any leftovers.
7. Bake for 15 minutes or so until slightly browned on top.
8. Top with avocado slices and garnish with coriander leaves. Serve and enjoy!

MEXICAN STREET CORN

Ingredients

- 4 ears of corn
- extra virgin olive oil
- sea salt
- cayenne pepper

Ingredients for the Chipotle Mayo

- ¼ cup vegan mayo
- 1 chipotle pepper in adobo sauce
- 1 tbsp. lime juice
- fresh cilantro to garnish

Directions

1. Drizzle shucked corn with olive oil and sprinkle with sea salt and a small dash of cayenne pepper.
2. Place on a hot grill and rotate a quarter of a turn ever 2-3 minutes until corn is tender and has light grill marks, around 10 minutes.
3. Meanwhile, place mayo, chipotle pepper in adobo sauce and lime juice in a food processor. Blend until creamy.
4. Drizzle hot corn with chipotle mayo and garnish with fresh cilantro leaves.

MEXICAN BLACK BEAN STEW RECIPE WITH AMARANTH GRAIN

Ingredients

- 4 cups vegetable broth
- 2 tbsp. olive oil
- 1 1/2 cups dried black beans (soak overnight in 4 cups of water)
- 2 large tomatoes
- 1 cup amaranth
- 1/2 + 1/2 teaspoon salt
- 3 cloves garlic, finely chopped
- 1 yellow beet, peeled and chopped (red is fine in a pinch)
- 1 tbsp. cumin
- 1 dried ancho chili (or New Mexican red chili)
- 1 red onion, finely chopped
- 1 bell pepper, finely chopped
- 2 shishito peppers or 1 jalapeño pepper, finely chopped
- 3 tbsp. smoky hot sauce (or Tabasco)
- 1/4 cup chopped cilantro
- 1 avocado, thinly sliced

Directions

1. First, soak the black beans overnight in a large pot covered by 2 inches of water. Rinse the beans a few times in cold water just before use and place the pot with the beans, 1 teaspoon salt and 4 cups of fresh water on the stove. Cover, cook over high heat until the water boils,

then reduce heat to a simmer. Cook for 40 minutes, then drain beans and set aside.

2. Roughly chop the tomatoes on a dinner plate and slide all of the pieces, juices and seeds into a bowl. Using your hands or a wooden spoon, smash the mixture until you have only small 1-inch pieces floating in tomato juice.

3. Rinse the amaranth in a small bowl under cold water. Add 1 cup amaranth to 3 cups water in a saucepan with a lid. Bring to a boil and then simmer for 20 minutes or until most of the water has been absorbed. Set aside.

4. In a large pot with a lid or Dutch oven, heat the olive oil over medium high heat. Add the onion, garlic, chopped beets, shishito and red peppers and 1/2 teaspoon salt. Cook for 5 minutes then add the cumin and crumble the chili into the pot, discarding the stem. Add the tomatoes and juice to the pot and cook for 5 more minutes, stirring occasionally.

5. Add the black beans and vegetable broth to the pot and bring the stew to a boil. Then add the amaranth, turn down the heat to a simmer and cook for 25 minutes. Add the hot sauce just before serving and place a few slices of avocado and a sprinkle of cilantro in each bowl.

Mexican Cauliflower

Ingredients

- 1 head of cauliflower, separated into bite size florets
- 2 tbsp. coconut oil
- 1 yellow onion, diced
- 1 small green bell pepper, diced
- 1 can (15 oz.) diced tomatoes with juice
- 1/8 tsp. ground cloves
- 1 tbsp. chili powder
- 1 tsp. ground cinnamon
- 1/2 teaspoon salt
- 1/4 teaspoon black pepper
- 1/4 cup fresh breadcrumbs
- 1/4 cup grated nondairy cheddar cheese, the grated kind

Directions

1. Lightly oil a 9" x 10" casserole dish and steam the cauliflower florets for 15 minutes. They will be done when easily pierced with a fork.
2. Heat oil in a large skillet. Sauté the onion and bell pepper for about 10 to 15 minutes or until the onion looks translucent.
3. Stir in the tomatoes and cook 5 minutes.
4. Add the spices and cook 3 more minutes.
5. Put the cauliflower in the prepared casserole. Pour all of the mixture from the skillet on top of the cauliflower.
6. Combine the breadcrumbs and nondairy cheese and sprinkle over the casserole.

7. Bake at 350° for 15 minutes.
8. Put under broiler for 1 minutes to brown up the top. Watch very closely.

Vegan Mexican Quinoa Bowl

Ingredients

- 2 Red Peppers
- 1 White Onion
- 1 Lime
- 1/4 - 1/2 Tsp. of Cayenne Pepper (depending on how spicy you like it!)
- 1 tsp. of Paprika
- 1 tsp. of Garlic Powder
- 1 Portion of my Perfect Guacamole

Ingredients for the Quinoa

- 2 Cups of Cooked Quinoa (In Stock)
- 1/2 Red Onion
- 1 Large Tomato
- 1 Large Handful of Coriander
- 1 Lime

Directions

1. Add a little coconut oil to a pan on medium heat. Slice your peppers and onions in to thin strips and add then add them to the pan.
2. Sprinkle in all the spices and give everything a good toss. Then leave it to cook, tossing occasionally, while you make the rest. -
3. Dice your red onion and tomato. Tear the coriander leaves from their stalks and give them a rough chop.

4. Add the red onion, coriander, tomato and cooked quinoa to a bowl and squeeze on the juice of half a lime. Toss it all together.
5. When the onions and peppers are soft and starting to brown, squeeze on the juice of half a lime and toss around once more.
6. Let cook for another minute or so and then take off the heat.
7. Divide the quinoa and peppers and onions between the two bowls, add a generous serving of guacamole and serve with a squeeze of extra lime.

BEER BEAN-STUFFED PEPPERS

Ingredients for beer beans

- ½ pound dried black beans, picked over and rinsed (or 2 cans of cooked beans; you'll need about 4 cups, cooked)
- 1 tsp. olive oil
- 1 yellow onion, chopped
- 2 cloves garlic, minced
- 12 ounces Mexican
- 1 canned chipotle Chile in adobo, chopped (1 pepper, not the whole can!), or ½ teaspoon chipotle Chile powder
- scant ½ teaspoon ground cinnamon
- sea salt

Ingredients for Peppers

- 6 poblano chilies
- 1 cup crumbled cotija or feta cheese
- 1 cup shredded Jack cheese
- juice of ½ lime
- 1 cup cherry tomatoes, chopped
- 1 tbsp. olive oil
- ½ cup chopped fresh cilantro

Directions

1. In a large bowl, soak the beans in plenty of water for at least 6 hours, or up to overnight.
2. Drain the beans and set them aside. In a large pot over medium heat, add the olive oil, onion and garlic and sauté for a few minutes, until the onion is just softened.

3. Add the soaked beans and 2½ cups water, stir, and bring the beans to a simmer. Simmer until the beans are cooked through (but not totally tender), 45 minutes to 75 minutes.
4. Add the beer, chipotle and cinnamon and simmer until much of the liquid is absorbed, around 20 minutes. If necessary, add some water to keep the beans from drying out.
5. Add ½ to ¾ teaspoon salt, to taste, and cook for another 10 minutes. Preheat the oven to 425 degrees and set the beans aside. Grease a large baking dish or cast iron skillet.
6. Cut a slit down the length of each poblano. Use your fingers (you might wear gloves) and a paring knife to remove, and then discard, the membranes and seeds from each pepper.
7. In a bowl, mix together the shredded Jack and crumbled cotija/feta cheese with the lime juice. If there is still a good amount of liquid in your beans, drain off some of it.
8. Mix the chopped tomatoes into the beans. Use a spoon to fill most of each pepper with beans, and then stuff a handful of cheese inside. Brush the outside of each pepper with olive oil and bake for around 25 minutes, until the tops are roasted and golden and the pepper is tender all around.
9. Serve peppers immediately, with the slit side up and garnished with cilantro.

SWEET POTATO BURRITOS

Ingredients

- 1 tbsp. vegetable oil
- 1 onion, chopped
- 4 cloves garlic, minced
- 6 cups canned kidney beans, drained
- 2 cups water
- 3 tbsp. chili powder
- 4 tsp prepared mustard
- 2 tsp ground cumin
- 1 pinch cayenne pepper, or to taste
- 2 tbsp. soy sauce
- +4 cups mashed cooked sweet potatoes
- 12 (10 inch) flour tortillas, warmed
- 8 ounces shredded Cheddar cheese

Directions

1. Preheat oven to 350 degrees F (175 degrees C).
2. Heat oil in a medium skillet and sauté onion and garlic until soft. Mash beans into the onion mixture.
3. Gradually stir in water; heat until warm, 2 to 3 minutes. Remove from heat and stir in the soy sauce, chili powder, mustard, cumin, and cayenne pepper.
4. Divide bean mixture and mashed sweet potatoes evenly between the tortillas; top with cheese.
5. Fold tortillas burrito-style around the fillings and place on a baking sheet.

6. Bake in the preheated oven until warmed through, about 12 minutes.

Chapter 3: Desserts

Minted Poached Peaches

Ingredients

- 6 firm, ripe peaches
- 2 cups sugar
- 1 vanilla bean, split (or 1/2 teaspoon pure vanilla extract)
- 2 strips lemon zest
- 1 large mint sprig, plus more for serving
- 4 cups water

Directions

1. Using a paring knife, lightly score an X into bottom of peaches (this will help with peeling later).
2. In a large saucepan, combine sugar, vanilla, lemon zest, mint, and water.
3. Cook over medium, stirring occasionally, until sugar has dissolved, about 2 minutes.
4. Add peaches and enough water to cover.
5. Bring to a bare simmer, and cook, turning occasionally, until peaches are easily pierced with a skewer, 6 to 10 minutes, depending on ripeness of peaches.
6. Remove peaches with a slotted spoon; let cool slightly.
7. Using a paring knife, peel peaches; return to syrup.

8. Serve with mint sprigs.

CHOCOLATE-COVERED BANANAS

Ingredients

- 8 ounces semisweet chocolate, chopped
- 6 popsicle sticks or wooden skewers
- 2 bananas, peeled and cut crosswise into thirds
- 1/3 cup coarsely chopped salted peanuts

Directions

1. Place chocolate in a heatproof bowl set over (not in) a pan of gently simmering water.
2. Stir just until melted.
3. Line a baking sheet with waxed paper. Insert a popsicle stick in one end of each banana piece.
4. Dip banana, one piece at a time, in chocolate, spooning on additional chocolate to cover.
5. Sprinkle each banana with peanuts, and set on prepared baking sheet.
6. Refrigerate until chocolate is firm, 20 minutes, or up to 3 days.

VEGAN MEXICAN CHOCOLATE SWEET POTATO PUDDING

Ingredients

- 1½ cups packed cooked mashed orange sweet potatoes (I used 2 smaller ones to get enough)
- ½ cup non-dairy milk (cashew, soy or "lite" coconut will all work, creamy is best)
- 5 tbsp. coconut sugar (32 g)
- ½ tbsp. strong cinnamon (I use Saigon)
- 1/16th-1/8 teaspoon cayenne (use to taste or omit if you don't want spicy, a little goes a long way)
- 1 tsp. vanilla extract
- ¼ tsp. fine sea salt
- ¼ tsp. Pure Liquid Alcohol-Free Stevia or other sweetener

Directions

1. Bake the sweet potatoes on parchment paper on a pan, not directly on the oven rack, at 400 degrees for 45 minutes to an hour. Depending on the size, the time will vary. You want them squishy soft (possible baking them over microwaving because they will preserve more flavor and more moisture).
2. Let your sweet potatoes cool and peel the skins.
3. Mash completely and then measure 1½ cups packed and leveled off. Add to a food processor. Process until smooth.

4. Add the remaining ingredients and process for a couple of minutes until completely smooth.
5. Scrape down the sides well and process once more.
6. Taste and adjust if needed.
7. Chill in a container for a couple of hours or more before eating.
8. You could eat it immediately if you like, but it firms up a bit more and tastes better cold, like regular pudding does.

Mexican Chocolate Cake

Ingredients

- 1 1/2 cups all-purpose flour
- 1 cups sugar
- 1/2 cup unsweetened cocoa powder
- 2 tsp. cinnamon
- 1 teaspoon baking soda
- 1/4 teaspoon cayenne pepper or chili powder
- 1/4 tsp. salt
- 1 tbsp. balsamic vinegar
- 1 tbsp. vanilla extract
- 1 cup cold water
- 2/3 cup powdered sugar
- 1/3 cup unsweetened cocoa powder
- 2 or 3 tbsp. water

Directions

1. Preheat oven to 350°F.
2. In a large mixing bowl, whisk together first seven ingredients (flour through salt). Make two small wells in the mixture. In one, pour in the vinegar. In the other, pour in the vanilla extract.
3. Pour cold water over everything. Stir until moistened and only a little lumpy.
4. Pour batter into an 8-inch round cake pan.
5. Bake for 30 or 35 minutes, or until a toothpick inserted in the center of the cake comes out clean.
6. Cool for 10 minutes in the pan, then carefully pry out and finish cooling on a wire rack.

7. While cake is baking, whisk together 2/3 cup powdered sugar and 1/3 cup unsweetened cocoa powder in small bowl.
8. Add water. Stir to make a thick glaze.
9. When cake is completely cooled, drizzle over cake

Mexican Chocolate Cupcakes

Ingredients for the cake

- 1 1/2 cups gluten-free all-purpose flour
- 1 cup sugar
- 1/3 cup unsweetened cocoa powder
- 1 tsp. baking soda
- 1/2 tsp. salt
- 1 tsp. cinnamon
- 3/4 tsp. xanthan gum
- 1/2 cup unsweetened almond milk
- 1/2 cup coffee (room temperature)
- 1/2 cup canola oil
- 2 tbsp. apple cider vinegar
- 2 tsp. pure vanilla extract

Ingredients for the frosting

- 1 cup original Earth Balance margarine
- 3 tbsp. unsweetened cocoa powder
- 2 1/2 cups powdered sugar
- 2 tbsp. unsweetened almond milk
- 1 ounce melted dark chocolate
- 1 tsp. pure vanilla extract
- pinch of cayenne pepper, to taste

Directions

1. Preheat oven to 350 degrees and line a cupcake tin with 12 paper liners.
2. In a large bowl, mix together all the dry ingredients (flour, sugar, baking soda, xanthan gum, salt, cinnamon)

3. In a separate bowl, mix together all the wet ingredients (milk, oil, vanilla, coffee, vinegar). Add the wet ingredients to the dry and mix until there are no clumps of dry ingredients but try not to over mix or the cakes won't rise as much
4. Bake for about 18 minutes, or until a toothpick inserted into the center of the cake comes out clean with just a few crumbles of cake on it Set the cakes aside and let them cool completely before frosting
5. In a medium bowl, beat together the "butter" with 1 tablespoon of cocoa powder. Add the rest of the cocoa powder and milk and beat until smooth
6. Add the powdered sugar one cup at a time, taste testing as you go.
7. Add in the vanilla extract and melted chocolate and incorporate. Add a pinch or two of cayenne pepper, tasting until you get it to your liking
8. Using a spatula, stuff a pastry bag full of frosting and swirl on top of each cupcake (if you don't have a pastry bag just using the spatula to put the frosting directly on the cupcakes will work – it just won't have the same look as the ones pictured here)
9. Dust each cupcake with a hint of cayenne pepper and enjoy!

Mexican Chocolate Lime Pudding Tarts

Ingredients for the crust

- 1 cup coconut
- ½ cup almonds
- 1 tbsp. cocoa
- 1 cup dates, pitted
- 1 tsp. agave nectar
- zest from one lime

Ingredients for the filling

- 1½ large avocados (about 2 cups)
- 2 tbsp. cocoa
- 4 tbsp. agave nectar
- ½ cup coconut cream
- ¼ tsp chili pepper
- 1 tsp vanilla extract
- ¼ tsp sea salt
- juice from one lime

Ingredients for the topping

- 1½ cups Coconut Whipped Cream
- Dark Chocolate bar for chocolate shavings

Directions for the crust

1. Add dates to food processor and process on high until date ball forms, about 30-40 seconds.

2. Add almonds and process for 1 minute, until almonds are chopped but still chunky.
3. Add remaining crust ingredients and process until well combined and the dough starts to stick together, about 2-3 minutes
4. Form crust into mini tart pans that are lined with plastic wrap (this will help make it easier to pull them back out after). Press down firmly into the tart pans and ensure evenly distributed.
5. Place tarts into freezer while you make the pudding mixture. Rinse out food processor bowl.

Directions for the pudding

1. Add avocados, lime juice, cocoa, agave nectar, coconut cream, chili pepper, vanilla and sea salt into processor bowl. Process on high for 2-3 minutes, scraping down sides as needed, until well blended and smooth.
2. Remove crusts from freezer and pop out of tart pans by lifting up on the plastic wrap.
3. Fill each tart crust with pudding, ensuring that the pudding mix is evenly distributed amongst the crusts.

Directions for the topping

1. Top each tart with approximately ½ cup Coconut Whipped Cream.
2. Using a citrus zester, zest dark chocolate over the coconut whipped cream layer until the

desired amount of chocolate shavings have been dusted over the tarts.

Arroz con Leche {Mexican Rice Pudding}

Ingredients

- ¾ Cup Raw Cashews
- ½ Cup Water
- 1 Cup Short Grain White Rice
- 2 Cups Water
- 3 Cups Soy Milk
- ¼ tsp. Sea Salt
- 2 Long Strips Orange Zest
- 1 Large Cinnamon Stick, preferably Mexican Canela
- ⅓ Cup Sugar
- Ground Cinnamon, preferably Mexican Canela for garnish

Directions

1. Soak the cashews in water for at least 2 hours. Drain the cashews and transfer to a blender. Add the ½ cup of water and blend until smooth. Set aside.
2. Heat a large saucepan or pot over medium heat and add the rice and 2 cups water. Bring to a boil and cook until most of the water has evaporated, stir often, about 5 minutes.
3. When most of the water has evaporated, add the soy milk, sea salt, orange zest, cinnamon stick and the blended cashew cream.
4. Bring a boil over medium heat, add in the sugar. Reduce to a low simmer.

5. Stir the rice often, making sure that the rice doesn't stick to the bottom of the pan. Cook until the rice is tender, about 20-30 minutes.
6. Remove from heat and take out the orange zest and cinnamon stick.
7. Let the rice cool a few minutes before serving.
8. Transfer to serving bowls and top with ground cinnamon.

MEXICAN CHOCOLATE ICE CREAM

Ingredients

- 2 (13.5 ounce) cans coconut milk, unsweetened
- ¼ cup agave nectar or honey
- 1 cup chocolate chunks
- 1 tbsp. ground cinnamon, ground
- Pinch Celtic sea salt
- ¼ tsp. cayenne (if you don't want a super spicy ice cream, then just use a pinch)
- 1 tsp decaf espresso, ground
- 1 tbsp. vanilla extract

Directions

1. In a medium saucepan, heat coconut milk and agave to a boil.
2. Reduce immediately to a simmer, then remove from heat.
3. Mix in the chocolate, stirring constantly until chips are. completely melted
4. Cool mixture in pan on counter for 1 hour.
5. Stir in the cinnamon, salt, cayenne, espresso and vanilla until thoroughly combined.
6. Add mixture to your ice cream maker, following directions per your machine.

Vegan Empanadas de Calabaza

Ingredients for filling

- 5-6 cups (40-50 oz.) uncooked pumpkin pieces (one sugar pumpkin will be enough)
- 5 cups water
- 1 tsp. cinnamon powder
- 1/2 tsp. anise grounded seeds
- 1/2 cup coconut sugar, add more if you like a sweeter filling

Ingredients for dough

- 2 cups Bob's Red Mill Oat Flour, gluten free
- 1/2 tsp. sea salt
- 2 tbsp. oil
- 10 tbsp. cold water

Directions for filling

1. Wash and cut sugar pumpkin into pieces.
2. Place water in a 5 quart cooking pot.
3. Place one layer of pumpkin pieces with skin side down.
4. Place second layer of pumpkin pieces with skin side facing up.
5. Bring to a boil on medium heat.
6. Lower heat to low and cover.
7. Cook for 1 hour.
8. If pumpkin has not softened, cook for an additional 30 minutes.
9. When done, let cool for five minutes.

10. Carefully remove pumpkin pieces from pot onto a baking sheet pan to cool.

11. Place a large metal strainer over a large bowl.

12. Remove pulp from pumpkin pieces and place in metal strainer.

13. Press pulp with a spoon and remove 1 cup of liquid.

14. In a medium saucepan, place pumpkin pulp, cinnamon, anise, and coconut sugar. Blend well.

15. Bring to a boil on medium heat.

16. Lower heat to low and cook for 1/2 an hour or until liquid has evaporated. Stir occasionally during this time.

17. Set aside to cool.

Directions for dough

1. Blend flour and salt in a medium mixing bowl.

2. Blend in oil until evenly distributed.

3. Add water and mix until water is absorbed.

4. Divide dough into 8 balls.

5. Place ball between two layers of plastic and press down with a pie plate. Make round about 4 1/2 to 5 inches in diameter.

6. Place 2 Tablespoons of pumpkin filling in the center of the round.

7. Bring one side of round and press down on the center edge to seal.

8. Press down along the edge to seal empanada completely. Remove excess filling.

9. Place all empanadas on a baking sheet pan that is lightly oiled or lined with a silicone mat.

10. Bake empanadas for 20 minutes at 350

11. Carefully remove empanadas to a cooling rack.

ONE LAST THING...

If you enjoyed this book or found it useful I'd be very grateful if you'd post a short review on Amazon.

Your support really does make a difference and I read all the reviews personally so I can get your feedback and make this book even better.

Thanks again for your support!

CPSIA information can be obtained
at www.ICGtesting.com
Printed in the USA
FSOW04n0911201216
28749FS